I0796575

This IS why You BARF

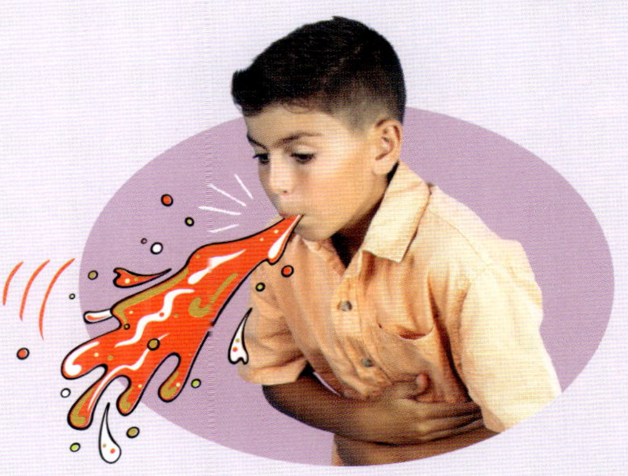

Dana Peabody

An imprint of PHOENIX International Publications, Inc.

Artwork © Shutterstock 2025 Pixoode; pakww; Roquillo Tebar; One Time; svtdesign; robuart; OkanNshgl; Aratehortua; berkut; Saroj Khuendee; Magi Bagi; RaymondZ; shutting; Mr.Yotsaran; Tommy Alven; Sudowoodo; Katakari; mw_atp5; Pikovit; Andrey_Popov; Lobanova; Ruben Pinto; Leestudio; xpixel; Elena Dijour; Anatoliy Karlyuk; Sunny studio; eveleen; Lemberg Vector studio; Pavel Aleks; Volodymyr Krasyuk; irin-k; Fotoinspiracja; Master1305; Andrey_Kuzmin; etorres; Maks Peoplenko; topseller; matin

Published by Sequoia Kids Media,
an imprint of Sequoia Publishing & Media, LLC

Sequoia Publishing & Media, LLC,
a division of Phoenix International Publications, Inc.

8501 West Higgins Road, Chicago, Illinois 60631
34 Seymour Street, London W1H 7JE
Heimhuder Straße 81, 20148 Hamburg

CustomerService@PhoenixInternational.com

www.PhoenixInternational.com

Library of Congress Control Number: 2024952391

ISBN: 979-8-7654-1135-3

This Is Why You BARF

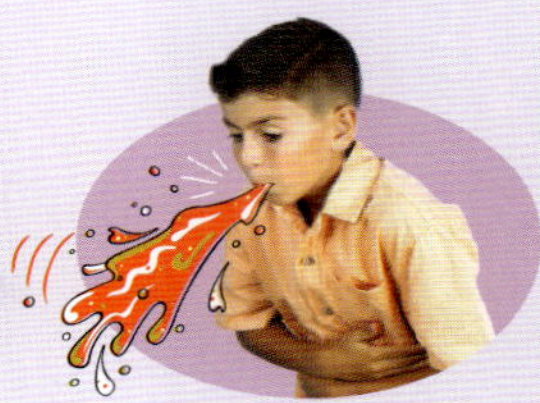

Table of Contents

Bold words are explained in the glossary.

Are you Feeling Queasy?

Sometimes, your stomach starts to feel funny...and you feel something rising in your body...

GULP!

...then you...

BARF!

But why and how does this happen? There are lots of different things that might make you throw up. Here are some examples.

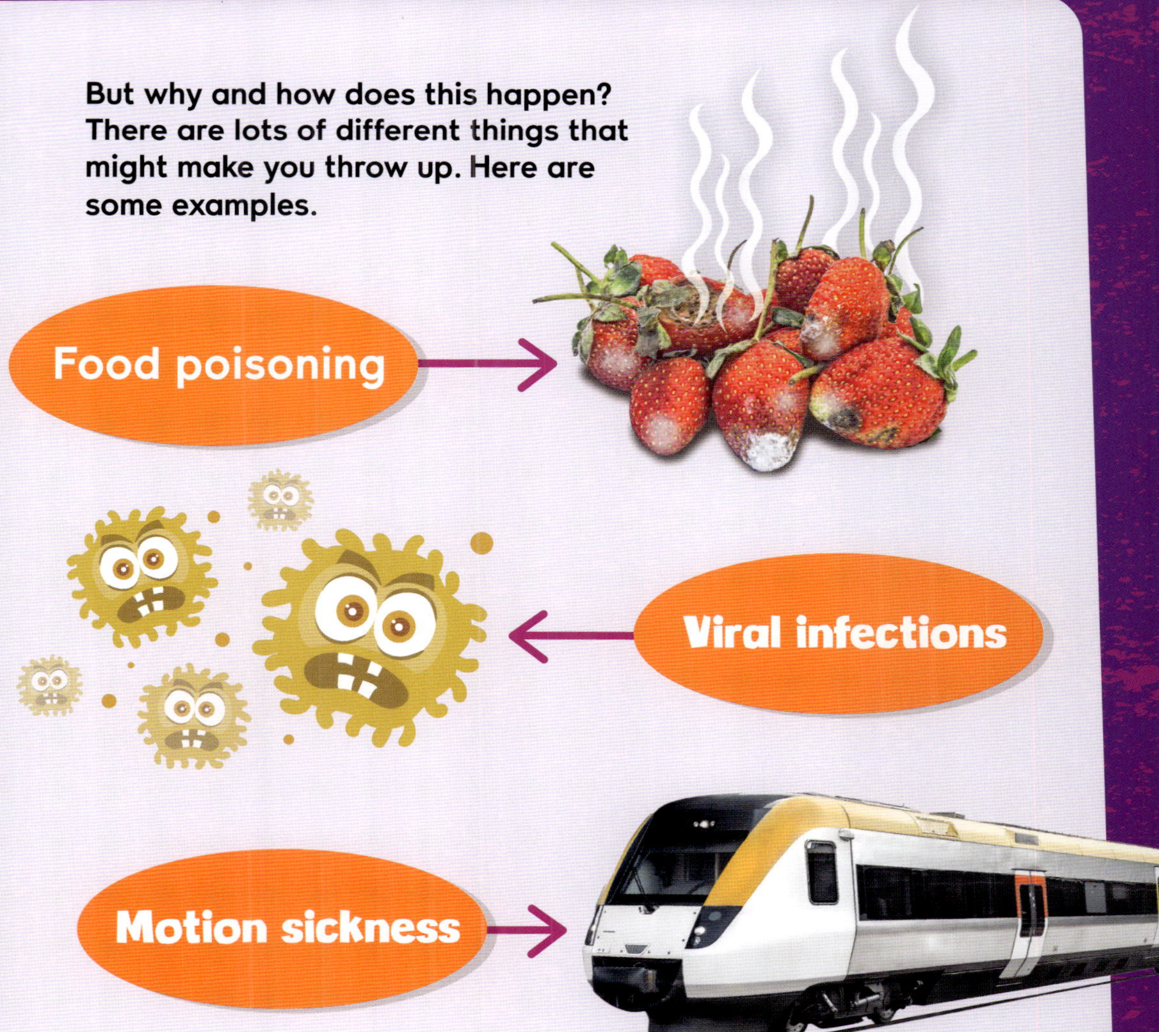

Gagging and Retching

Before you actually barf, you might gag or heave. This is when the **muscles** inside your body **contract** and **relax** over and over again.

These contractions make anything inside your stomach move around quickly.

Sometimes you can gag and heave and not be sick. This might happen because you have seen or smelled something really gross.

Sometimes seeing someone else barf can make you want to barf as well!

Digestion Gone Wrong

The digestive system usually moves food downwards through your body, **filtering** all the **nutrients** from your food. But when you are going to barf, everything goes a bit topsy-turvy...

Start at Stage 1 and follow the barf all the way back up the body!

Stage 3:

The barf then comes out of your MOUTH—with a top speed of around 62 feet (18 meters) per second!

Stage 1:

First, anything in your INTESTINES is pushed back into the stomach.

Stage 2:

Then it is pushed out of the STOMACH and into the ESOPHAGUS (uh-soff-a-gus).

You can get food poisoning from eating food that has expired, or food that has been **contaminated** with bad **bacteria**.

Your body will do everything it can to get the bad food out.

Food poisoning might make you barf lots, have diarrhea (die-ah-ree-ah), or run a fever. These will either kill the bad bacteria or get them out of your body.

Viruses

Viral infections, such as stomach flu, are highly **contagious** and can make you barf—a lot!

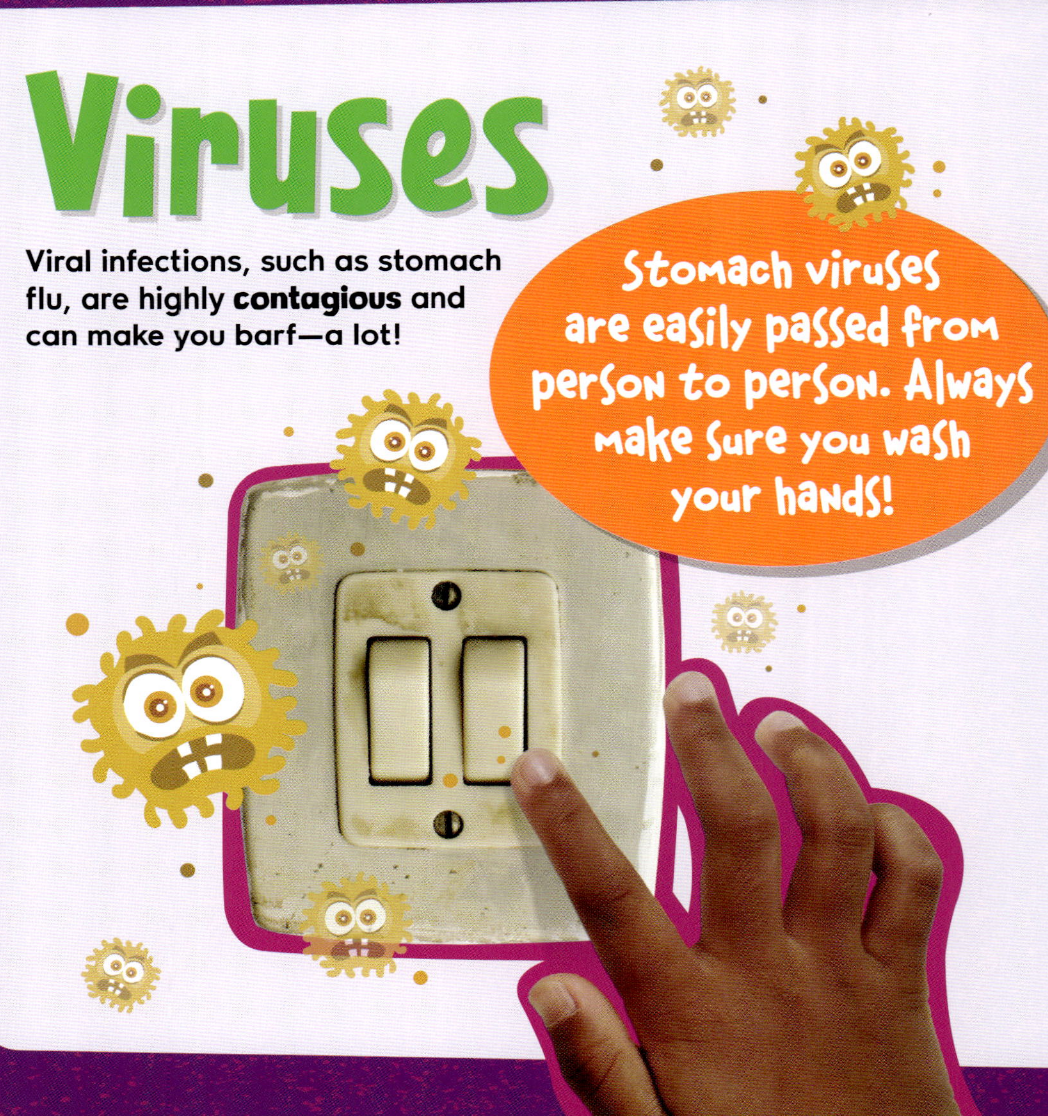

When you are sick, contagious **particles** are spread far and wide. Scientists even made a robot called Vomiting Larry to show just how far these particles travel.

Theme Park Puke

If you go on a rollercoaster or travel in a car, train, or plane, then you might feel (or even be) sick. This is because of motion sickness.

If you can feel movement, but your eyes can't see that you are moving (or the other way around), your body can get confused and feel sick.

Sore Throats and Blocked Noses

When you throw up, the vomit can come out of both your mouth and your nose. This is because the esophagus is connected to both!

Sometimes barf is traveling so fast, it has to come out of both the nose and mouth!

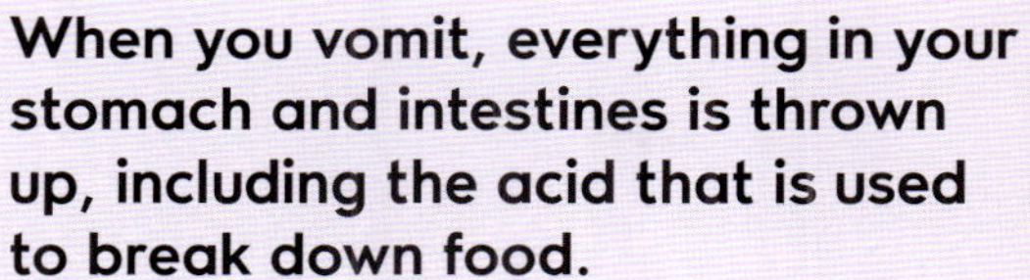

When you vomit, everything in your stomach and intestines is thrown up, including the acid that is used to break down food.

This acid can make your throat and nose sore as it comes out of your body.

Stomach acid

Funky and Chunky

Barf can be different colors and different textures depending on what you ate or drank and how digested your food is.

If you are sick right after eating, you will see chunks of that food in your vomit.

For example, if you have just eaten a red lollipop and then you are sick, your barf will probably have bits of red lollipop in it!

PEE-EW!

Parmesan cheese and barf smell very similar because they both contain the same type of acid.

Houseflies vomit on their food to make it easier for them to eat!

If a dog throws up, it might eat its own barf. The dog uses its excellent sense of smell to find tasty bits of food left in the vomit!

People can have a fear of barfing or seeing other people barf. This is called emetophobia.

Test Your Knowledge

Can you match the food with the barf?

Answers: A. 2; B. 3; C. 4; D. 1

Glossary

bacteria: microscopic living things that can cause diseases

contagious: (of a disease) able to spread from one person to another

contaminated: to have made something unclean by adding a poisonous or polluting substance to it

contract: (of muscles) to become shorter or smaller through tightening

filtering: removing unwanted materials by passing through something, like a strainer

motion sickness: feeling sick or nauseous while traveling or moving

muscles: bundles of tissue that can contract or squeeze together

nutrients: natural substances that people need to grow and stay healthy

particles: extremely small pieces of a substance

relax: (of muscles) to become longer and bigger by not being tensed

square foot: a measurement of an area that is a square with each side being a foot in length

viral infections: illnesses that are caused by a virus being inside the body

Index